13.35q

Meet the Family
My Sister

by Mary Auld

Gareth Stevens Publishing
A WORLD ALMANAC EDUCATION GROUP COMPANY

This is Sally and her sister Kate with their mom and dad. Sally is three years younger than Kate.

Brian's sister is much older than he is. Sometimes she takes care of him.

Brianna and Louise are identical twins. Only their mom and dad can tell which sister is which.

Anne has a new baby sister, Lucy. Lucy has a different mom than Anne, so she is her half sister.

Nicky and Ruby are best friends and stepsisters. They have different parents, but now Ruby's dad is married to Nicky's mom.

Kevin and his sister go to the same school, but they are in different classes.

Mary's sister is on
a soccer team.

Miguel's sister paints very well. Sometimes she lets Miguel help.

Lizzie tickles her sister.

William makes his sister giggle.

Leo and his sister play
games together.

Mel and her sisters
like putting on shows
for their parents.

This is Nina
with her mom
and her Aunt
Janet. Aunt
Janet is Nina's
mom's sister.

Do you have a sister?
What is she like?

Family Words

Here are some words people use when talking about their sister or family.

Names for children:
sister, brother, daughter, son.

Names for parents:
**father, daddy, dad, papa,
mother, mommy, mom, mama.**

Names of other relatives:
**grandchild, grandparent,
grandmother, grandma,
grandfather, grandpa,
uncle, aunt, nephew, niece.**

A step relative is a person who is related
by a parent's remarriage, not by birth.

A half brother and a half sister are related
to each other by only one parent.

A Family Tree

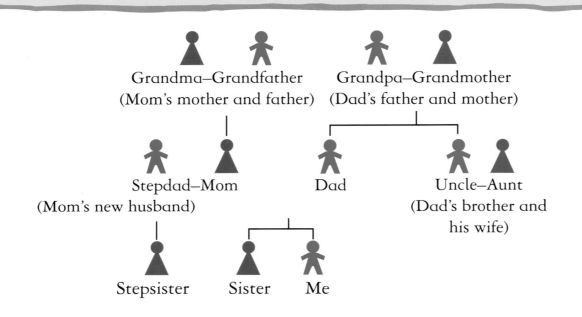

Grandma–Grandfather
(Mom's mother and father)

Grandpa–Grandmother
(Dad's father and mother)

Stepdad–Mom
(Mom's new husband)

Dad

Uncle–Aunt
(Dad's brother and
his wife)

Stepsister

Sister

Me

You can show how you are related to all your family
on a plan like this one. It is called a family tree.
Every family tree is different. Try drawing your own.

Please visit our web site at: www.garethstevens.com
For a free color catalog describing Gareth Stevens Publishing's list of high-quality
books and multimedia programs, call 1-800-542-2595 (USA) or 1-800-387-3178
(Canada). Gareth Stevens Publishing's fax: (414) 332-3567.

Library of Congress Cataloging-in-Publication Data available upon request from publisher.
Fax (414) 336-0157 for the attention of the Publishing Records Department.

ISBN 0-8368-3928-5

This North American edition first published in 2004 by Gareth Stevens Publishing,
A World Almanac Education Group Company, 330 West Olive Street, Suite 100,
Milwaukee, WI 53212 USA

This U.S. edition copyright © 2004 by Gareth Stevens, Inc. First published in 2003 by
Franklin Watts, 96 Leonard Street, London EC2A 4XD. Original copyright © 2003 by
Franklin Watts.

Series editor: Rachel Cooke
Art director: Jonathan Hair
Design: Andrew Crowson
Gareth Stevens editor: Betsy Rasmussen
Gareth Stevens art direction: Tammy Gruenewald

Picture Credits: Paul Baldesare/Photofusion: 13. Bruce Berman/Corbis: front cover main, 22.
www.johnbirdsall.co.uk: front cover center below, 2, 5. Dex Images Inc/Corbis: 1, 14. Paul
Doyle/Photofusion: 16. Jon Feingersch/ Corbis: 12. Carlos Goldin/Corbis: front cover center
above. Sally Greenhill, Sally & Richard Greenhill: 6, 11, 20-21. Ronnie Kauffman/Corbis:
8-9. Roy McMahon/Corbis: 18. Jose Luis Pelaez/Corbis: front cover center top. George Shelley/
Corbis: front cover bottom. Ariel Skelley/Corbis: front cover center. Paula Solloway/Format:
17. Mo Wilson/Format: 19. While every attempt has been made to clear copyright, should
there be any inadvertent omission please notify the publisher regarding rectification.

Printed in Hong Kong/China

1 2 3 4 5 6 7 8 9 08 07 06 05 04